I0014631

Disclaimer

The information provided within this eBook is for general informational purposes only. While we try to keep the information up-to-date and correct, there are no representations or warranties, express or implied, about the completeness, accuracy, reliability, suitability or availability with respect to the information, products, services, or related graphics contained in this eBook for any purpose.

©Mumbai

Computer Shortcut keys and Tricks - Word, Excel , Power Point, Internet , trouble shooting and Everything

Table of Contents

Microsoft Excel shortcut keys

Shortcut Keys   Description

F2   Edit the selected cell.

F5   Go to a specific cell. For example, C6.

F7   Spell check selected text or document.

F11   Create chart.

Ctrl + Shift + ;   Enter the current time.

Ctrl + ;   Enter the current date.

Alt + Shift + F1 Insert New Worksheet.

Shift + F3   Open the Excel formula window.

Shift + F5   Bring up search box.

Ctrl + A Select all contents of the worksheet.

Ctrl + B Bold highlighted selection.

Ctrl + I Italic highlighted selection.

Ctrl + K Insert link.

Ctrl + U Underline highlighted selection.

Ctrl + 5 Strikethrough highlighted selection.

Ctrl + P Bring up the print dialog box to begin printing.

Ctrl + Z Undo last action.

Ctrl + F9   Minimize current window.

Ctrl + F10   Maximize currently selected window.

Ctrl + F6   Switch between open workbooks / windows.

Ctrl + Page up   Move between Excel work sheets in the same Excel document.

Ctrl + Page down   Move between Excel work sheets in the same Excel document.

Ctrl + Tab   Move between Two or more open Excel files.

Alt + = Create a formula to sum all of the above cells

Ctrl + ' Insert the value of the above cell into cell currently selected.

Ctrl + Shift + !   Format number in comma format.

Ctrl + Shift + $ Format number in currency format.

Ctrl + Shift + #   Format number in date format.

Ctrl + Shift + %   Format number in percentage format.

Ctrl + Shift + ^   Format number in scientific format.

Ctrl + Shift + @   Format number in time format.

Ctrl + Arrow keyMove to next section of text.

Ctrl + Space   Select entire column.

Shift + Space   Select entire row.

Microsoft Word shortcut keys

Shortcut Keys   Description

Ctrl + 0 Adds or removes 6pts of spacing before a paragraph.

Ctrl + A Select all contents of the page.

Ctrl + B Bold highlighted selection.

Ctrl + C Copy selected text.

Ctrl + E Aligns the line or selected text to the center of the screen.

Ctrl + F Open find box.

Ctrl + I Italic highlighted selection.

Ctrl + J Aligns the selected text or line to justify the screen.

Ctrl + K Insert link.

Ctrl + L Aligns the line or selected text to the left of the screen.

Ctrl + MIndent the paragraph.

Ctrl + P Open the print window.

Ctrl + R Aligns the line or selected text to the right of the screen.

Ctrl + T Create a hanging indent.

Ctrl + U Underline highlighted selection.

Ctrl + V Paste.

Ctrl + X Cut selected text.

Ctrl + Y Redo the last action performed.

Ctrl + Z Undo last action.

Ctrl + Shift + L   Quickly create a bullet point.

Ctrl + Shift + F   Change the font.

Ctrl + Shift + >   Increase selected font +1pts up to 12pt and then increases font +2pts.

Ctrl +] Increase selected font +1pts.

Ctrl + Shift + <   Decrease selected font -1pts if 12pt or lower, if above 12 decreases font by +2pt.

Ctrl + [Decrease selected font -1pts.

Ctrl + / + c   Insert a cent sign (¢).

Ctrl + ' + <char> Insert a character with an accent (grave) mark, where <char> is the character you want. For example, if you wanted an accented è you would use Ctrl + ' + e as your shortcut key. To reverse the accent mark use the opposite accent mark, often on the tilde key.

Ctrl + Shift + *   View or hide non printing characters.

Ctrl + <left arrow>   Moves one word to the left.

Ctrl + <right arrow>   Moves one word to the right.

Ctrl + <up arrow>   Moves to the beginning of the line or paragraph.

Ctrl + <down arrow>   Moves to the end of the paragraph.

Ctrl + Del   Deletes word to right of cursor.

Ctrl + Backspace   Deletes word to left of cursor.

Ctrl + End   Moves the cursor to the end of the document.

Ctrl + Home   Moves the cursor to the beginning of the document.

Ctrl + Spacebar Reset highlighted text to the default font.

Ctrl + 1 Single-space lines.

Ctrl + 2 Double-space lines.

Ctrl + 5 1.5-line spacing.

Ctrl + Alt + 1   Changes text to heading 1.

Ctrl + Alt + 2   Changes text to heading 2.

Ctrl + Alt + 3   Changes text to heading 3.

Alt + Ctrl + F2   Open new document.

Ctrl + F1   Open the Task Pane.

Ctrl + F2   Display the print preview.

Ctrl + Shift + > Increases the highlighted text size by one.

Ctrl + Shift + < Decreases the highlighted text size by one.

Ctrl + Shift + F6 Opens to another open Microsoft Word document.

Ctrl + Shift + F12   Prints the document.

F1   Open Help.

F4   Repeat the last action performed (Word 2000+)

F5   Open the find, replace, and go to window in Microsoft Word.

F7   Spellcheck and grammar check selected text or document.

F12   Save as.

Shift + F3   Change the text in Microsoft Word from uppercase to lowercase or a capital letter at the beginning of every word.

Shift + F7   Runs a Thesaurus check on the word highlighted.

Shift + F12   Save.

Shift + Enter   Create a soft break instead of a new paragraph.

Shift + Insert   Paste.

Shift + Alt + D   Insert the current date.

Shift + Alt + T   Insert the current time.

Mouse shortcuts.

Mouse shortcuts   Description

Click, hold, and drag   Selects text from where you click and hold to the point you drag and let go.

Double-click   If double-click a word, selects the complete word.

Double-click   Double-clicking on the left, center, or right of a blank line will make the alignment of the text left, center, or right aligned.

Double-click   Double-clicking anywhere after text on a line will set a tab stop.

Triple-click   Selects the line or paragraph of the text the mouse triple-clicked.

Ctrl + Mouse wheel   Zooms in and out of document.

Shutdown Command Via Command Prompt

The 'Shutdown' Command Becomes More Flexible and Automated when used from the Command Prompt.

To Run the 'Shutdown' command from the command prompt, go to 'Start > Run', type 'cmd', and press 'Enter'.

In the black box (the command prompt) type 'Shutdown' and the Switches you want to use with the 'Shutdown' command.

You have to use at least one switch for the shutdown command to work.

The Switches :-

The 'Shutdown' command has a few options called Switches. You can always see them by typing 'shutdown -?' in the command prompt if you forget any of them.

-i: Display GUI interface, must be the first option

-l: Log off (cannot be used with -m option)

-s: Shutdown the computer

-r: Shutdown and restart the computer

-a: Abort a system shutdown

-m \\computername: Remote computer to shutdown/restart/abort

-t xx: Set timeout for shutdown to xx seconds

-c "comment": Shutdown comment (maximum of 127 characters)

-f: Forces running applications to close without warning

-d [u][p]:xx:yy: The reason code for the shutdown u is the user code p is a planned shutdown code xx is the major reason code (positive integer less than 256) yy is the minor reason code (positive integer less than 65536)

Note :- I've noticed using a switch with a '-' sign doesn't work sometimes.

If you are having trouble try using a '/' in place of '-' in your switches.

Examples :-

shutdown –m \\computername –r –f

This command will restart the computer named computername and force any programs that might still be running to stop.

shutdown –m \\computername –r –f –c "I'm restarting your computer. Please save your work now." –t 120

This command will restart the computer named computername, force any programs that might still be running to stop, give to user on that computer a message, and countdown 120 seconds before it restarts.

shutdown –m \\computername –a

This command will abort a previous shutdown command that is in progress.

Using A Batch File :-
You can create a file that performs the shutdown command on many computers at one time.

In this example I'm going to create a batch file that will use the shutdown command to shut down 3 computers on my home network before I go to bed.

Open 'Notepad' and type the shutdown command to shut down a computer for each computer on the network.

Make sure each shutdown command is on its own line.

An example of what should be typed in notepad is given below-

shutdown –m \\computer1 –s

shutdown –m \\computer2 –s

shutdown –m \\computer3 -s

Now I'll save it as a batch file by going to file, save as, change save as type to all files, give the file a name ending with '.bat'. I named mine 'shutdown.bat'.

Pick the location to save the batch file in and save it.

When you run the batch file it'll shutdown computer 1, 2, and 3 for you.

You can use any combination of shutdown commands in a batch file.

Calculations On Command Prompt

-: Calculations On Command Prompt :-

The command processor CMD.EXE comes with a mini-calculator that can perform simple arithmetic on 32-bit signed integers: C:\>set /a 2+2

4

C:\>set /a 2*(9/2)

8

C:\>set /a (2*9)/2

9

C:\>set /a "31>>2"

7

Note that we had to quote the shift operator since it would otherwise be misinterpreted as a "redirect stdout and append" operator.

For more information, type set /? at the command prompt.

Google Chrome tips, tricks and shortcuts

1. Create desktop and Start menu shortcuts to web apps such as Gmail - go to Gmail.com and then select Create application shortcuts... from the Page Control menu (in the top-right corner of your browser - it looks like a page with the corner folded over). Now choose where you want to place your shortcut. This works for other Google apps such as Calendar and Documents, and other services such as Windows Live Hotmail.

2. Control + Shift + N opens an 'incognito' window - sites you view in this window won't appear in your history and cookies served by sites in this window will be deleted when the window is closed.

3. You can open a link in an incognito window by right-clicking the link and selecting Open link in incognito window.

4. Alt + Home loads your Google Chrome home page, with thumbnails of your most visited sites shown in the active tabbed window.

5. Control + T opens a new tab. You can drag tabs around to change their order or drag a tab out of the window into its own window.

6. Control + Shift + T opens your most recently closed tab. Press the key combination again to open the tab closed before that one. Google Chrome remembers the last 10 tabs you've closed.

7. Jump to different open tabs using Control + 1, Control + 2, Control + 3, etc. Control + 9 takes you to the last tab.

8. Control + Tab lets you cycle through your open tabs in order.

9. Control + Shift + Tab cycles through your tabs in the opposite order.

10. As with Firefox 3, you can drag a link onto a tab to open it in that tab, or drop it between two tabs to open a new tab in that position.

11. To bookmark a site click the star on the left of the address bar and then select a folder to add it to.

12. Control +B hides the Google Chrome bookmarks bar. Press Control + B to bring it back again.

13. Right-click or hold down the back button and you'll get a drop-down list of sites to go back through. Show Full History, at the bottom of the list, opens a new tab with your full browser history.

14. Control + H is a faster way to bring up the History page.

15. You can delete history for chosen days by scrolling to the day you want to delete and clicking Delete history for this day on the right-hand side of the window.

16. Control + J brings up your Downloads page.

17. To clear an item from your Downloads page, right-click an entry and select Remove.

18. Press Control + K or Control + E to search from the address bar. Once pressed, you'll see a ? symbol appear in the address bar and you can simply enter your search query and hit Return.

19. Right-click the top of the browser window and select Task manager to see how much memory different tabs and plug-ins are using. Highlight one and click End process to stop it running.

20. Shift + Escape is a quicker way to bring up the Google Chrome Task manager.

21. To see what plug-ins are installed, type about:plugins into the address window.

22. You can also type the following commands into the Google Chrome address window: about:stats, about:network, about:histograms, about:memory, about:cache, about:dns.

23. Type about:crash to see what a crashed tab looks like.

24. A three-second diversion: type about:internets. (Only works in Windows XP.)

25. Edit any web page - right-click a page and select Inspect element. Now edit the HTML source code and hit Return to view the changes.

26. To make Google Chrome your default browser, click the Tools button (in the right-hand corner of the browser window - a spanner icon). Select Options, click the Basics tab and then click the Make Google Chrome my default browser button.

27. To delete cookies, go to Tools > Options > Under the Hood. Scroll down to the Security section, and click Show cookies. Now you can click Remove all or remove individual cookies.

28. To clear more data such as the Google Chrome browsing history and cache, click the Tools icon and select Clear browsing data...

29. To clear the most visited web sites that appear on your Google Chrome start page, you must clear your browsing history using the method above.

30. Clearing your Google Chrome browser history will also stop matches from previously browsed sites appearing as suggestions in your address bar.

Internet Explorer 8 keyboard shortcuts

Internet Explorer 8 keyboard shortcuts

To do this

Press this

Display Help

F1

Toggle between full-screen and regular views of the browser window

F11

Move forward through the items on a webpage, the Address bar, or the Favorites bar

TAB

Move back through the items on a webpage, the Address bar, or the Favorites bar

SHIFT+TAB

Start Caret Browsing

F7

Go to your home page

ALT+HOME

Go to the next page

ALT+RIGHT ARROW

Go to the previous page

ALT+LEFT ARROW or BACKSPACE

Display a shortcut menu for a link

SHIFT+F10

Move forward through frames and browser elements

CTRL+TAB or F6

Scroll toward the beginning of a document

UP ARROW

Scroll toward the end of a document

DOWN ARROW

Scroll toward the beginning of a document in larger increments

PAGE UP

Scroll toward the end of a document in larger increments

PAGE DOWN

Move to the beginning of a document

HOME

Move to the end of a document

END

Find on this page

CTRL+F

Refresh the current webpage

F5

Refresh the current webpage, even if the time stamp for the web version and your locally stored version are the same

CTRL+F5

Stop downloading a page

ESC

Open a new website or page

CTRL+O

Open a new window

CTRL+N

Open a new InPrivate Browsing window

CTRL+SHIFT+P

Duplicate tab (open current tab in a new tab)

CTRL+K

Reopen the last tab you closed

CTRL+SHIFT+T

Close the current window (if you only have one tab open)

CTRL+W

Save the current page

CTRL+S

Print the current page or active frame

CTRL+P

Activate a selected link

ENTER

Open Favorites

CTRL+I

Open History

CTRL+H

Open Feeds

CTRL+J

Open the Page menu

ALT+P

Open the Tools menu

ALT+T

Open the Help menu

ALT+H

Working with tabs

The following table describes shortcuts used when working with tabs.

To do this

Press this

Open links in a new tab in the background

CTRL+click

Open links in a new tab in the foreground

CTRL+SHIFT+click

Open a new tab in the foreground

CTRL+T

Switch between tabs

CTRL+TAB or CTRL+SHIFT+TAB

Close current tab (or the current window if tabbed browsing is disabled)

CTRL+W

Open a new tab in the foreground from the Address bar

ALT+ENTER

Switch to a specific tab number

CTRL+n (where n is a number between 1 and 8)

Switch to the last tab

CTRL+9

Close other tabs

CTRL+ALT+F4

Toggle Quick Tabs (thumbnail view) on or off

CTRL+Q

Using zoom

The following table describes shortcuts used for zooming.

To do this

Press this

Increase zoom (+ 10%)

CTRL+PLUS SIGN

Decrease zoom (- 10%)

CTRL+MINUS SIGN

Zoom to 100%

CTRL+0

Using search

The following table describes shortcuts used for search.

To do this

Press this

Go to the search box

CTRL+E

Open your search query in a new tab

ALT+ENTER

Open the search provider menu

CTRL+DOWN ARROW

Using Print Preview

The following table describes shortcuts used to preview and print webpages.

To do this

Press this

Set printing options and print the page

ALT+P

Change paper, headers and footers, orientation, and margins for this page

ALT+U

Display the first page to be printed

ALT+HOME

Display the previous page to be printed

ALT+LEFT ARROW

Type the number of the page you want displayed

ALT+A

Display the next page to be printed

ALT+RIGHT ARROW

Display the last page to be printed

ALT+END

Specify how you want frames to print (this option is available only if you are printing a webpage that uses frames)

ALT+F

Close Print Preview

ALT+C

Using the Address bar

The following table describes shortcuts used on the Address bar.

To do this

Press this

Select the text in the Address bar

ALT+D

Display a list of addresses you've typed

F4

When in the Address bar, move the cursor left to the next logical break in the address (period or slash)

CTRL+LEFT ARROW

When in the Address bar, move the cursor right to the next logical break in the address (period or slash)

CTRL+RIGHT ARROW

Add "www." to the beginning and ".com" to the end of the text typed in the Address bar

CTRL+ENTER

Move forward through the list of AutoComplete matches

UP ARROW

Move back through the list of AutoComplete matches

DOWN ARROW

Opening Internet Explorer toolbar menus

The following table describes shortcuts used to open Internet Explorer toolbar and Command bar menus.

To do this

Press this

Open the Home menu

ALT+M

Open the Print menu

ALT+R

Open the RSS menu

ALT+J

Open the Tools menu

ALT+O

Open the Safety menu

ALT+S

Open the Help menu

ALT+L

Working with feeds, history, and favorites

The following table describes shortcuts used when working with feeds, history, and favorites.

To do this

Press this

Add the current page to your favorites (or subscribe to the feed when in feed preview)

CTRL+D

Delete browsing history

CTRL+SHIFT+DEL

Open an InPrivate Browsing window

CTRL+SHIFT+P

Open the Organize Favorites dialog box

CTRL+B

Move selected item up in the Favorites list in the Organize Favorites dialog box

ALT+UP ARROW

Move selected item down in the Favorites list in the Organize Favorites dialog box

ALT+DOWN ARROW

Open Favorites Center and display your favorites

ALT+C

Open Favorites Center and display your history

CTRL+H

Open Favorites Center and display your feeds

CTRL+J

Open and dock the Favorites Center and display your feeds

CTRL+SHIFT+J

Open the Add to Favorites menu (or open Subscribe to feed when in feed preview)

ALT+Z

Open the Favorites menu from the menu bar

ALT+A

Display all feeds (when in feed view)

ALT+I

Mark a feed as read (when in feed view)

ALT+M

Put cursor in Search box in feed view

ALT+S

Editing

The following table describes shortcuts used when editing webpages.

To do this

Press this

Remove the selected items and copy them to the Clipboard

CTRL+X

Copy the selected items to the Clipboard

CTRL+C

Insert the contents of the Clipboard at the selected location

CTRL+V

Select all items on the current webpage

CTRL+A

Open Internet Explorer Developer Tools

F12

Using the Information bar

The following table describes shortcuts used when working with the Information bar.

To do this

Press this

Move focus to the Information bar

ALT+N

Click the Information bar

SPACEBAR

Window and Tab Shortcuts

Action/Function   Shortcut

Open a new window   Ctrl + N

Open a new windows in incognito mode Ctrl + Shift + N

Open link in a new tab   Ctrl + Click on link

Open link in new window   Shift + Click on link

Close current window   Alt + F4

Open a new tab Ctrl + T

Reopen the last tab you've closed1   Ctrl + Shift + T

Switch to the tab at the specified position   Ctrl + 1 through Ctrl + 8

Switch to the last tab   Ctrl + 9

Switch to the next tab   Ctrl + Tab or Ctrl + PgDown

Switch to the previous tab   Ctrl + Shift + Tab or Ctrl + PgUp

Go to the previous page in your browsing history for the tab   Backspace, or press Alt + Left Arrow

Go to the next page in your browsing history for the tab Shift + Backspace, or press Alt + Right Arrow

Close current tab or pop-up   Ctrl + W or Ctrl + F4

Open your homepage   Alt + Home

Open a file from your computer in Google Chrome   Ctrl + O, then select file

1 Google Chrome remembers the last 10 tabs that you've closed

Action/Function	Shortcut
Add 'www.' and '.com' to your input in the address bar and open the web address	Type the part of the web address that's between 'www.' and '.com', then press Ctrl + Enter
Highlight content in the web address area	F6 or Ctrl + L or Alt + D
Open your web address in a new tab	Type a web address, then press Alt + Enter
Places a '?' in the address bar. Type a search term after the '?' to perform a search using your default search engine.	Ctrl + K or Ctrl + E
Jump to the previous word in the address bar	Place your cursor in the address bar, the press Ctrl + Left Arrow
Jump to the next word in the address bar	Place your cursor in the address bar, then press Ctrl + Right Arrow
Delete the previous word in the address bar	Place your cursor in the address bar, then press Ctrl + Backspace

Action/Function	Shortcut
Toggle bookmarks bar on and off	Ctrl + B
View the History page	Ctrl + H
View the Downloads page	Ctrl + J
View the Task Manager	Shift + Esc

Action/Function	Shortcut
Print your current page	Ctrl + P
Reload current page	F5
Stop page loading	Esc
Reload current page, ignoring cached content	Ctrl + F5 or Shift + F5
Scroll down the web page	Space bar
Go to the top of the page	Home
Go to the bottom of the page	End
Download link	Press Alt, then click the link

Open find-in-page box   Ctrl + F

Find next match for your input in the find-in-page box   Ctrl + G or F3

Find previous match for your input in the find-in-page box   Ctrl + Shift + G or Shift + F3

View source   Ctrl + U

Bookmark your current webpage   `Ctrl + D

Make text larger   Ctrl + +

Make text smaller   Ctrl + -

Return to normal text size   Ctrl + 0

Action/Function   Shortcut

Copy content to the clipboard   Highlight content, then press Ctrl + C

Paste current content from the clipboard   Place your cursor in a text field, then press Ctrl + V or Shift + Insert

Delete the content and copy it to the clipboard (cut)   Highlight the content in a text field, then press Ctrl + X or Shift + Delete

Mozilla Firefox shortcut keys

Mozilla Firefox shortcut keys

Below is a listing of all the major shortcut keys in Mozilla Firefox.

Shortcut Keys   Description

Alt + Home   Go to home page.

Alt + Left Arrow Back a page.

Backspace   Back a page.

Alt + Right Arrow   Forward a page.

F5   Refresh current page, frame, or tab.

F11   Display the current website in full screen mode. Pressing F11 again will exit this mode.

Esc   Stop page or download from loading.

Ctrl + (- or +)   Increase or decrease the font size, pressing '-' will decrease and '+' will increase.

Shift + Enter   Complete a .net instead of a .com address.

Ctrl + Shift + Enter   Complete a .org address.

Ctrl + Shift + DelOpen the Clear Data window to quickly clear private data.

Ctrl + D Add a bookmark for the page currently opened.

Ctrl + I Display available bookmarks.

Ctrl + J Display the download window.

Ctrl + N Open New browser window.

Ctrl + P Print current page / frame.

Ctrl + T Opens a new tab.

Ctrl + F4 or Ctrl + W   Closes the currently selected tab.

Ctrl + Shift + T   Undo the close of a window.

Ctrl + Tab   Moves through each of the open tabs.

Spacebar   Moves down a page at a time.

Shift + SpacebarMoves up a page at a time.

Alt + Down arrow   Display all previous text entered in a text box and available options on drop down menu.

Shortcuts for windows

about: ->show version info

about:version -> same to about:

about:cache -> show cache content

about:plugins -> show info of plugins installed

about:memory ->show memory usage

about:crash -> crash the tab

about:dns -> show dns info, like time

about:network -> network tools

about:stats -> shh! this page is secret!

about:internets -> the tubes are clogged!

about:histograms ->histograms resume

Window and tab shortcuts

Ctrl+N Open a new window

Ctrl+Shift+N Open a new window in incognito mode

Press Ctrl, and click a link Open link in a new tab

Press Shift, and click a link Open link in a new window

Alt+F4 Close current window

Ctrl+T Open a new tab

Ctrl+Shift+T Reopen last tab closed (remembers 10)

Drag link to tab Open link in specified tab

Drag link to space between tabs Open link in a new tab

Ctrl+1 through Ctrl+8 Switch to the tab at the specified position number. The number you press represents a position on the tab strip.

Ctrl+9 Switch to the last tab

Ctrl+Tab or Ctrl+PgDown Switch to the next tab

Ctrl+Shift+Tab or Ctrl+PgUp Switch to the previous tab

Ctrl+W or Ctrl+F4 Close current tab or pop-up

Alt+Home Open your homepage

Ctrl+O, then select file Open a file from your computer in Google Chrome

Address bar shortcuts

Do one of the following actions in the address bar:

Type a search term Perform a search using your default search engine

Type the part of the web address that's between 'www.' and '.com', then press Ctrl+Enter

Type a search engine keyword or URL, press Tab, then type a search term Perform a search using the search engine associated with the keyword or the URL. Google Chrome prompts you to press Tab if it recognizes the search engine you're trying to use.

F6 or Ctrl+L or Alt+D Highlight content in the web address area

Type a web address, then press Alt+Enter Open your web address in a new tab

Shortcuts to open Google Chrome features

Ctrl+B Toggle bookmarks bar on and off

Ctrl+H View the History page

Ctrl+J View the Downloads page

Shift+Escape View the Task manager

Webpage shortcuts

Ctrl+P Print your current page

F5 Reload current page

Esc Stop page loading

Ctrl+F5 or Shift+F5 Reload current page, ignoring cached content

Press Alt, and click a link Download link

Ctrl+F Open find-in-page box

Ctrl+G or F3 Find next match for your input in the find-in-page box

Ctrl+Shift+G or Shift+F3 Find previous match for your input in the find-in-page box

Ctrl+U View source

Drag link to bookmarks bar Bookmark the link

Ctrl+D Bookmark your current webpage

Ctrl++ Make text larger

Ctrl+- Make text smaller

Ctrl+0 Return to normal text size

Other

Backspace, or press Alt and the left arrow together Go to the previous page in your browsing history for the tab

Shift+Backspace, or press Alt and the right arrow togetherGo to the next page in your browsing history for the tab

Ctrl+K or Ctrl+E Places a '?' in the address bar. Type a search term after the '?' to perform a search using your default search engine.

Place your cursor in the address bar, then press Ctrl and the left arrow together Jump to the previous word in the address bar

Place your cursor in the address bar, then press Ctrl and the right arrow together Jump to the next word in the address bar

Place your cursor in the address bar, then press Ctrl+Backspace Delete the previous word in the address bar

Space bar Scroll down the web page

Home Go to the top of the page

End Go to the bottom of the page

General keyboard shortcuts

General keyboard shortcuts

CTRL+C (Copy)

CTRL+X (Cut)

CTRL+V (Paste)

CTRL+Z (Undo)

DELETE (Delete)

SHIFT+DELETE (Delete the selected item permanently without placing the item in the Recycle Bin)

CTRL while dragging an item (Copy the selected item)

CTRL+SHIFT while dragging an item (Create a shortcut to the selected item)

F2 key (Rename the selected item)

CTRL+RIGHT ARROW (Move the insertion point to the beginning of the next word)

CTRL+LEFT ARROW (Move the insertion point to the beginning of the previous word)

CTRL+DOWN ARROW (Move the insertion point to the beginning of the next paragraph)

CTRL+UP ARROW (Move the insertion point to the beginning of the previous paragraph)

CTRL+SHIFT with any of the arrow keys (Highlight a block of text)

SHIFT with any of the arrow keys (Select more than one item in a window or on the desktop, or select text in a document)

CTRL+A (Select all)

F3 key (Search for a file or a folder)

ALT+ENTER (View the properties for the selected item)

ALT+F4 (Close the active item, or quit the active program)

ALT+ENTER (Display the properties of the selected object)

ALT+SPACEBAR (Open the shortcut menu for the active window)

CTRL+F4 (Close the active document in programs that enable you to have multiple documents open simultaneously)

ALT+TAB (Switch between the open items)

ALT+ESC (Cycle through items in the order that they had been opened)

F6 key (Cycle through the screen elements in a window or on the desktop)

F4 key (Display the Address bar list in My Computer or Windows Explorer)

SHIFT+F10 (Display the shortcut menu for the selected item)

ALT+SPACEBAR (Display the System menu for the active window)

CTRL+ESC (Display the Start menu)

ALT+Underlined letter in a menu name (Display the corresponding menu)

Underlined letter in a command name on an open menu (Perform the corresponding command)

F10 key (Activate the menu bar in the active program)

RIGHT ARROW (Open the next menu to the right, or open a submenu)

LEFT ARROW (Open the next menu to the left, or close a submenu)

F5 key (Update the active window)

BACKSPACE (View the folder one level up in My Computer or Windows Explorer)

ESC (Cancel the current task)

SHIFT when you insert a CD-ROM into the CD-ROM drive (Prevent the CD-ROM from automatically playing)

CTRL+SHIFT+ESC (Open Task Manager)

Dialog box keyboard shortcuts

If you press SHIFT+F8 in extended selection list boxes, you enable extended selection mode. In this mode, you can use an arrow key to move a cursor without changing the selection. You can press CTRL+SPACEBAR or SHIFT+SPACEBAR to adjust the selection. To cancel extended selection mode, press SHIFT+F8 again. Extended selection mode cancels itself when you move the focus to another control.

CTRL+TAB (Move forward through the tabs)

CTRL+SHIFT+TAB (Move backward through the tabs)

TAB (Move forward through the options)

SHIFT+TAB (Move backward through the options)

ALT+Underlined letter (Perform the corresponding command or select the corresponding option)

ENTER (Perform the command for the active option or button)

SPACEBAR (Select or clear the check box if the active option is a check box)

Arrow keys (Select a button if the active option is a group of option buttons)

F1 key (Display Help)

F4 key (Display the items in the active list)

BACKSPACE (Open a folder one level up if a folder is selected in the Save As or Opendialog box)

Microsoft natural keyboard shortcuts

Windows Logo (Display or hide the Start menu)

Windows Logo+BREAK (Display the System Properties dialog box)

Windows Logo+D (Display the desktop)

Windows Logo+M (Minimize all of the windows)

Windows Logo+SHIFT+M (Restore the minimized windows)

Windows Logo+E (Open My Computer)

Windows Logo+F (Search for a file or a folder)

CTRL+Windows Logo+F (Search for computers)

Windows Logo+F1 (Display Windows Help)

Windows Logo+ L (Lock the keyboard)

Windows Logo+R (Open the Run dialog box)

Windows Logo+U (Open Utility Manager)

Accessibility keyboard shortcuts

Right SHIFT for eight seconds (Switch FilterKeys either on or off)

Left ALT+left SHIFT+PRINT SCREEN (Switch High Contrast either on or off)

Left ALT+left SHIFT+NUM LOCK (Switch the MouseKeys either on or off)

SHIFT five times (Switch the StickyKeys either on or off)

NUM LOCK for five seconds (Switch the ToggleKeys either on or off)

Windows Logo +U (Open Utility Manager)

Windows Explorer keyboard shortcuts

END (Display the bottom of the active window)

HOME (Display the top of the active window)

NUM LOCK+Asterisk sign (*) (Display all of the subfolders that are under the selected folder)

NUM LOCK+Plus sign (+) (Display the contents of the selected folder)

NUM LOCK+Minus sign (-) (Collapse the selected folder)

LEFT ARROW (Collapse the current selection if it is expanded, or select the parent folder)

RIGHT ARROW (Display the current selection if it is collapsed, or select the first subfolder)

Shortcut keys for Character Map

After you double-click a character on the grid of characters, you can move through the grid by using the keyboard shortcuts:

RIGHT ARROW (Move to the right or to the beginning of the next line)

LEFT ARROW (Move to the left or to the end of the previous line)

UP ARROW (Move up one row)

DOWN ARROW (Move down one row)

PAGE UP (Move up one screen at a time)

PAGE DOWN (Move down one screen at a time)

HOME (Move to the beginning of the line)

END (Move to the end of the line)

CTRL+HOME (Move to the first character)

CTRL+END (Move to the last character)

SPACEBAR (Switch between Enlarged and Normal mode when a character is selected)

Microsoft Management Console (MMC) main window keyboard shortcuts

CTRL+O (Open a saved console)

CTRL+N (Open a new console)

CTRL+S (Save the open console)

CTRL+M (Add or remove a console item)

CTRL+W (Open a new window)

F5 key (Update the content of all console windows)

ALT+SPACEBAR (Display the MMC window menu)

ALT+F4 (Close the console)

ALT+A (Display the Action menu)

ALT+V (Display the View menu)

ALT+F (Display the File menu)

ALT+O (Display the Favorites menu)

MMC console window keyboard shortcuts

CTRL+P (Print the current page or active pane)

ALT+Minus sign (-) (Display the window menu for the active console window)

SHIFT+F10 (Display the Action shortcut menu for the selected item)

F1 key (Open the Help topic, if any, for the selected item)

F5 key (Update the content of all console windows)

CTRL+F10 (Maximize the active console window)

CTRL+F5 (Restore the active console window)

ALT+ENTER (Display the Properties dialog box, if any, for the selected item)

F2 key (Rename the selected item)

CTRL+F4 (Close the active console window. When a console has only one console window, this shortcut closes the console)

Remote desktop connection navigation

CTRL+ALT+END (Open the Microsoft Windows NT Security dialog box)

ALT+PAGE UP (Switch between programs from left to right)

ALT+PAGE DOWN (Switch between programs from right to left)

ALT+INSERT (Cycle through the programs in most recently used order)

ALT+HOME (Display the Start menu)

CTRL+ALT+BREAK (Switch the client computer between a window and a full screen)

ALT+DELETE (Display the Windows menu)

CTRL+ALT+Minus sign (-) (Place a snapshot of the entire client window area on the Terminal server clipboard and provide the same functionality as pressing ALT+PRINT SCREEN on a local computer.)

CTRL+ALT+Plus sign (+) (Place a snapshot of the active window in the client on the Terminal server clipboard and provide the same functionality as pressing PRINT SCREEN on a local computer.)

Microsoft Internet Explorer navigation

CTRL+B (Open the Organize Favorites dialog box)

CTRL+E (Open the Search bar)

CTRL+F (Start the Find utility)

CTRL+H (Open the History bar)

CTRL+I (Open the Favorites bar)

CTRL+L (Open the Open dialog box)

CTRL+N (Start another instance of the browser with the same Web address)

CTRL+O (Open the Open dialog box, the same as CTRL+L)

CTRL+P (Open the Print dialog box)

CTRL+R (Update the current Web page)

CTRL+W (Close the current window)

Windows Short Cut Keys

Delete selected item permanently without placing the item in the Recycle Bin. SHIFT+DELETE

Create shortcut to selected item. CTRL+SHIFT while dragging an item

Rename selected item. F2

Move the insertion point to the beginning of the next word. CTRL+RIGHT ARROW

Move the insertion point to the beginning of the previous word. CTRL+LEFT ARROW

Move the insertion point to the beginning of the next paragraph. CTRL+DOWN ARROW

Move the insertion point to the beginning of the previous paragraph. CTRL+UP ARROW

Highlight a block of text. CTRL+SHIFT with any of the arrow keys

Select more than one item in a window or on the desktop, or select text within a document. SHIFT with any of the arrow keys

Select all. CTRL+A

Search for a file or folder. F3

View properties for the selected item. ALT+ENTER

Close the active item, or quit the active program. ALT+F4

Opens the shortcut menu for the active window. ALT+SPACEBAR

Close the active document in programs that allow you to have multiple documents open simultaneously. CTRL+F4

Switch between open items. ALT+TAB

Cycle through items in the order they were opened. ALT+ESC

Cycle through screen elements in a window or on the desktop. F6

Display the Address bar list in My Computer or Windows Explorer. F4

Display the shortcut menu for the selected item. SHIFT+F10

Display the System menu for the active window. ALT+SPACEBAR

Display the Start menu. CTRL+ESC (came before winkey)

Activate the menu bar in the active program. F10

Open the next menu to the right, or open a submenu. RIGHT ARROW

Open the next menu to the left, or close a submenu. LEFT ARROW

Refresh the active window. F5

View the folder one level up in My Computer or Windows Explorer. BACKSPACE

Cancel the current task. ESC

SHIFT when you insert a CD into the CD-ROM drive Prevent the CD from automatically playing.

Move forward through tabs. CTRL+TAB

Move backward through tabs. CTRL+SHIFT+TAB

Move forward through options. TAB

Move backward through options. SHIFT+TAB

Carry out the corresponding command or select the corresponding option. ALT+Underlined letter

Carry out the command for the active option or button. ENTER

Select or clear the check box if the active option is a check box. SPACEBAR

Select a button if the active option is a group of option buttons. Arrow keys

Display Help. F1

Display the items in the active list. F4

Open a folder one level up if a folder is selected in the Save As or Open dialog box. BACKSPACE

Display or hide the Start menu.

Display the System Properties dialog box. WINKEY+BREAK

Show the desktop. WINKEY+D

Minimize all windows. WINKEY+M

Restores minimized windows. WINKEY+Shift+M

Open My Computer. WINKEY+E

Search for a file or folder. WINKEY+F

Search for computers. CTRL+WINKEY+F

Display Windows Help. WINKEY+F1

Lock your computer if you are connected to a network domain, or switch users if you are not connected to a network domain. WINKEY+ L

Open the Run dialog box. WINKEY+R

Open Utility Manager. WINKEY+U

Helpful accessibility keyboard shortcuts:

Switch FilterKeys on and off. Right SHIFT for eight seconds

Switch High Contrast on and off. Left ALT +left SHIFT +PRINT SCREEN

Switch MouseKeys on and off. Left ALT +left SHIFT +NUM LOCK

Switch StickyKeys on and off. SHIFT five times

Switch ToggleKeys on and off. NUM LOCK for five seconds

Open Utility Manager. WINKEY+U

Keyboard shortcuts you can use with Windows Explorer:

Display the bottom of the active window. END

Display the top of the active window. HOME

Display all subfolders under the selected folder. NUM LOCK+ASTERISK on numeric keypad (*)

Display the contents of the selected folder. NUM LOCK+PLUS SIGN on numeric keypad (+)

Collapse the selected folder. NUM LOCK+MINUS SIGN on numeric keypad (-)

Collapse current selection if it's expanded, or select parent folder. LEFT ARROW

Display current selection if it's collapsed, or select first subfolder. RIGHT ARROW

Top 40 best Windows 7 keyboard shortcuts

Keyboard shortcuts have been a part of Windows for ages, but not before Windows 7 has there been a shortcut for just about anything and everything you want to do on the computer. We've gathered up what we feel the Top 40 Windows 7 keyboard shortcuts are for you in the hopes of easing your life just a little bit, and virtually never having to touch your mouse ever again.

Of course, all of this depends on your ability to remember all of these.

Alt + Enter: Display properties for the selected item.

Alt + Esc: Cycle through items in the order of which they were opened.

Alt + F4: Close the active item or exit the active program.

Alt + spacebar: Open the shortcut menu for the active window.

Alt + Tab: Shift between open programs.

Ctrl + A: Select all the items in a document or window.

Ctrl + C: Copy the selected item.

Ctrl + V: Paste the selected item.

Ctrl + X: Cut the selected item.

Ctrl + Y: Redo an action.

Ctrl + Z: Undo last action.

Ctrl + Shift + arrow key: Select a block of text.

Ctrl + Shift + N: Create a new folder anywhere on your computer where folders can be created.

Ctrl + Shift + Esc: Open Task Manager.

F1: Display help.

F2: Rename the selected item.

F5: Refresh the active window.

F6: Cycle through elements in a window or on the Desktop.

F10: Activate the menu bar in the current program.

Shift + Del: Delete an item without sending it to the Recycle Bin.

Shift + F10: Display the shortcut menu for the selected item.

Windows Key Keyboard Shortcuts

All of the following shortcuts involve using the Windows logo key which looks like this .

 : Open or close the Start menu.

 + B: Change from the Desktop to the System Tray, and then you can use the arrow keys to cycle through the items there.

 + E: Launch Windows Explorer/Computer.

 + F: Launch file and folder finder.

 + G: Cycle through gadgets.

 + M: Minimize all Windows for quick access to the desktop.

 + P: Quickly connect your computer to a projector or some other form of display.

 + R: Open the Run dialog box.

 + T: Cycle through programs on the Taskbar.

 + U: Open Ease of Access Center.

 + X: Open Windows Mobility Center.

 + down cursor arrow: Minimize the current program.

 + up cursor arrow: Maximize the current program window.

 + Home button: Minimize all windows except the current one.

 + Pause button: Display System Properties dialog box.

 + Shift + M: Restore minimized windows to the Desktop.

 + space bar: Shows you the desktop immediately.

 + Tab: Flip through the programs on the Taskbar using Aero Flip 3-D.

Ctrl + + B: Switch to the program that had a message appear in the status area

Some More General Shortcuts

The General Shortcuts

We'll kickoff the list with some really general shortcuts that you often used.

CTRL+C (Copy)

§ CTRL+X (Cut)

§ CTRL+V (Paste)

§ CTRL+Z (Undo)

§ Delete (Delete)

§ Shift+Delete (Delete the selected item permanently without placing the item in the Recycle Bin)

§ CTRL while dragging an item (Copy the selected item)

§ CTRL+Shift while dragging an item (Create a shortcut to the selected item)

§ F2 key (Rename the selected item)

§ CTRL+RIGHT ARROW (Move the insertion point to the beginning of the next word)

§ CTRL+LEFT ARROW (Move the insertion point to the beginning of the previous word)

§ CTRL+DOWN ARROW (Move the insertion point to the beginning of the next paragraph)

§ CTRL+UP ARROW (Move the insertion point to the beginning of the previous paragraph)

§ CTRL+Shift with any of the arrow keys (Highlight a block of text)

§ Shift with any of the arrow keys (Select more than one item in a window or on the desktop, or select text in a document)

§ CTRL+A (Select all)

§ F3 key (Search for a file or a folder)

§ Alt+Enter (View the properties for the selected item)

§ Alt+F4 (Close the active item, or quit the active program)

§ Alt+Enter (Display the properties of the selected object)

§ Alt+Spacebar (Open the shortcut menu for the active window)

§ CTRL+F4 (Close the active document in programs that enable you to have multiple documents open simultaneously)

§ Alt+Tab (Switch between the open items)

§ Alt+ESC (Cycle through items in the order that they had been opened)

§ F6 key (Cycle through the screen elements in a window or on the desktop)

§ F4 key (Display the Address bar list in My Computer or Windows Explorer)

§ Shift+F10 (Display the shortcut menu for the selected item)

§ Alt+Spacebar (Display the System menu for the active window)

§ CTRL+ESC (Display the Start menu)

§ Alt+Underlined letter in a menu name (Display the corresponding menu)

§ Underlined letter in a command name on an open menu (Perform the corresponding command)

§ F10 key (Activate the menu bar in the active program)

§ RIGHT ARROW (Open the next menu to the right, or open a submenu)

§ LEFT ARROW (Open the next menu to the left, or close a submenu)

§ F5 key (Update the active window)

§ Backspace (View the folder one level up in My Computer or Windows Explorer)

§ ESC (Cancel the current task)

§ Shift when you insert a CD-ROM into the CD-ROM drive (Prevent the CD-ROM from automatically playing)

§ CTRL+Tab (Move forward through the tabs)

§ CTRL+Shift+Tab (Move backward through the tabs)

§ Tab (Move forward through the options)

§ Shift+Tab (Move backward through the options)

§ Alt+Underlined letter (Perform the corresponding command or select the corresponding option)

§ Enter (Perform the command for the active option or button)

§ Spacebar (Select or clear the check box if the active option is a check box)

§ Arrow keys (Select a button if the active option is a group of option buttons)

§ F1 key (Display Help)

§ F4 key (Display the items in the active list)

§ Backspace (Open a folder one level up if a folder is selected in the Save As or Open dialog box)

§ Win (Display or hide the Start menu)

§ Win+BREAK (Display the System Properties dialog box)

§ Win+D (Display the desktop)

§ Win+M (Minimize all of the windows)

§ Win+Shift+M (Restore the minimized windows)

§ Win+E (Open My Computer)

§ Win+F (Search for a file or a folder)

§ CTRL+Win+F (Search for computers)

§ Win+F1 (Display Windows Help)

§ Win+ L (Lock the keyboard)

§ Win+R (Open the Run dialog box)

§ Win+U (Open Utility Manager)

§ Right Shift for eight seconds (Switch FilterKeys either on or off)

§ Left Alt+left Shift+PRINT SCREEN (Switch High Contrast either on or off)

§ Left Alt+left Shift+NUM LOCK (Switch the MouseKeys either on or off)

§ Shift five times (Switch the StickyKeys either on or off)

§ NUM LOCK for five seconds (Switch the ToggleKeys either on or off)

§ Win +U (Open Utility Manager)

§ END (Display the bottom of the active window)

§ HOME (Display the top of the active window)

§ NUM LOCK+* (Display all of the subfolders that are under the selected folder)

§ NUM LOCK++ (Display the contents of the selected folder)

§ NUM LOCK+- (Collapse the selected folder)

§ LEFT ARROW (Collapse the current selection if it is expanded, or select the parent folder)

§ RIGHT ARROW (Display the current selection if it is collapsed, or select the first subfolder)

§ After you double-click a character on the grid of characters, you can move through the grid by using the keyboard shortcuts:

§ RIGHT ARROW (Move to the right or to the beginning of the next line)

§ LEFT ARROW (Move to the left or to the end of the previous line)

§ UP ARROW (Move up one row)

§ DOWN ARROW (Move down one row)

§ PAGE UP (Move up one screen at a time)

§ PAGE DOWN (Move down one screen at a time)

§ HOME (Move to the beginning of the line)

§ END (Move to the end of the line)

§ CTRL+HOME (Move to the first character)

§ CTRL+END (Move to the last character)

§ Spacebar (Switch between Enlarged and Nor mal mode when a character is selected)

§ CTRL+O (Open a saved console)

§ CTRL+N (Open a new console)

§ CTRL+S (Save the open console)

§ CTRL+M (Add or remove a console item)

§ CTRL+W (Open a new window)

§ F5 key (Update the content of all console windows)

§ Alt+Spacebar (Display the MMC window menu)

§ Alt+F4 (Close the console)

§ Alt+A (Display the Action menu)

§ Alt+V (Display the View menu)

§ Alt+F (Display the File menu)

§ Alt+O (Display the Favorites menu)

§ CTRL+P (Print the current page or active pane)

§ Alt+- (Display the window menu for the active console window)

§ Shift+F10 (Display the Action shortcut menu for the selected item)

§ F1 key (Open the Help topic, if any, for the selected item)

§ F5 key (Update the content of all console windows)

§ CTRL+F10 (Maximize the active console window)

§ CTRL+F5 (Restore the active console window)

§ Alt+Enter (Display the Properties dialog box, if any, for the selected item)

§ F2 key (Rename the selected item)

§ CTRL+F4 (Close the active console window. When a console has only one console window, this shortcut closes the console)

§ CTRL+Alt+END (Open the m*cro$oft Windows NT Security dialog box)

§ Alt+PAGE UP (Switch between programs from left to right)

§ Alt+PAGE DOWN (Switch between programs from right to left)

§ Alt+INSERT (Cycle through the programs in most recently used order)

§ Alt+HOME (Display the Start menu)

§ CTRL+Alt+BREAK (Switch the client computer between a window and a full screen)

§ Alt+Delete (Display the Windows menu)

§ CTRL+Alt+- (Place a snapshot of the active window in the client on the Terminal server clipboard and provide the same functionality as pressing PRINT SCREEN on a local computer.)

§ CTRL+Alt++ (Place a snapshot of the entire client window area on the Terminal server clipboard and provide the same functionality as pressing Alt+PRINT SCREEN on a local computer.)

§ CTRL+B (Open the Organize Favorites dialog box)

§ CTRL+E (Open the Search bar)

§ CTRL+F (Start the Find utility)

§ CTRL+H (Open the History bar)

§ CTRL+I (Open the Favorites bar)

§ CTRL+L (Open the Open dialog box)

§ CTRL+N (Start another instance of the browser with the same Web address)

§ CTRL+O (Open the Open dialog box, the same as CTRL+L)

§ CTRL+P (Open the Print dialog box)

§ CTRL+R (Update the current Web page)

§ CTRL+W (Close the current window)

Viewing Your IP Address Information

There are several ways you can determine your IP address information:

IPCONFIG

Start / Run / cmd

IPCONFIG /ALL

This opens a command window. One advantage is that you can send the information to a text file (IPCONFIG /ALL > c:\ip.txt)

But sometimes the window shows show much information you need to scroll around to fine it.

VIEW STATUS

Control Panel / Network Connections / Double click the iconsfor your network (If the network has an icon in the system tray you can also just double click on that icon)

Click on the Support tab

Click on the Details button

The below basic shortcut keys are a listing of shortcut keys that will work with almost all PC compatible computers and software programs.

Shortcut Keys

Description

Alt + E

Edit options in current program

Alt + F

File menu options in current program

Ctrl + A

Select all text.

Ctrl + B Bolds the current (highlighted) selection

Ctrl + C

Copy selected item

Ctrl + C + C   Opens the clipboard

Ctrl + F

Find.

Ctrl + H Replace, brings up the Find and Replace dialog box.

Ctrl + I Add or remove Italic formatting.

Ctrl + P Print

Ctrl + S Save

Ctrl + U Add or remove Underline

Ctrl + W   Close

Ctrl + V

Paste copied item

Ctrl + X

Cut.

Ctrl + Y Redo last command

Ctrl + Z Undo last command

Ctrl + Ins

Same as Ctrl + c

Ctrl + left arrow

Move one word to the left at a time.

Ctrl + right arrow

Move one word to the right at a time.

Shift + Ins

Paste

Shift + Delelte or Del

Cut. Or permanently delete selected item(s) on Windows Explorer.

F1

Help.

Home

Jump to the beginning of the line or page.

Ctrl + Home

Jump to the beginning of the document or page.

End

Jump to the end of the line or page.

Ctrl + End

ump to the end of the document or page.

Shift + Home

Set selection (highlight) from current position to beginning of the line or page.

Shift + End

Set selection (highlight) from current position to end of the line or page.

Shift + left arrow

Set selection (highlight) from current position to the left, one character at a time.

Shift + right arrow

Set selection (highlight) from current position to the right, one character at a time.

Shift + down arrow

Set selection (highlight) from current position to the next line down.

Shift + up arrow

Set selection (highlight) from current position to the next line up.

Ctrl + = Spell checker